I0199150

TATTOOS

First published in 2024 by
The Dedalus Press
13 Moyclare Road
Baldoyle
Dublin D13 K1C2
Ireland

www.dedaluspress.com

Copyright © Eva Bourke, 2024

ISBN 978-1-915629-27-2 (paperback)
ISBN 978-1-915629-26-5 (hardback)

All rights reserved.
No part of this publication may be reproduced in any form
or by any means without the prior permission
of the publisher.

The moral rights of the author have been asserted.

Dedalus Press titles are available in Ireland
from Argosy Books (www.argosybooks.ie) and in the UK
from Inpress Books (www.inpressbooks.co.uk)

Cover artwork *Mountainside Cilin* by Miriam de Búrca,
by kind permission.

The Dedalus Press receives financial assistance from
The Arts Council / An Chomhairle Ealaíon.

TATTOOS

EVA BOURKE

DEDALUS PRESS

ACKNOWLEDGEMENTS

The author wishes to thank the publishers and editors of the following magazines and journals in which a number of these poems, or earlier versions of them, originally appeared: 'Jour Fixe', *The Irish Times;* 'A Line by Borges', *Cyphers,* ed. Eiléan Ní Chuilleanáin; 'Graveyards', *Tenemos,* ed. James Harpur; 'Dvořák in America', Commissioned for Galway Music Residency Creative Response Art, Poetry, Music on Film; 'Where Music Begins', Commissioned for *Micheál Ó Súilleabháin: A Life in Music.* ed. Helen Phelan; 'Twenty-Eight Swimmers', *Strokestown Anthology 2022,* ed. Margaret Hickey; 'The Earth Remembers', commissioned for *Bealach an Fhéir Ghortaigh / Hunger's Way,* a film by Edwina Guckian and Vincent Woods; 'Dear Jessie, when I think of us…' commissioned for *Days of Clear Light: A Festschrift in Honour of Jessie Lendennie and in Celebration of Salmon poetry at 40,* ed. Neassa O'Mahony; and 'Eroica', *Sunday Miscellany: A Selection 2018–2023,* ed. Sarah Binchy.

Contents

In the Second Year – from a Pandemic Journal / 71

for my loves, living and dead

What sings is what stays silent.
     —Adam Zagajewski

Soft air,
wet leaves:
— the scent was spring the scent sorrow.
          —Adam Zagajewski

Kite on the Beach

First thing, the dogs were upset,
running in circles on the sand,
barking, it seemed, at nothing,

then I noticed people looking up:
In the overcast sky way above
the kelp-strewn strand

a kite swayed and looped,
its spectral tail streaming behind it
in an updraught. I, too, looked up

as the kite climbed higher, grew smaller
and disappeared in the grey clouds
over the grey sea on a cold day in March.

Why did you come here, kite? I asked,
Is it to mock me, to brag of lightness
when I am rooted to the ground, weighed down by loss?

There was no answer, then sorrow flew in
on a crow's wing and said: All you see
are a cold house and silent vacant days.

But open your hands and heart to me,
take me into you like bitter food
and I will make you light.

Jour Fixe

So lasst mich scheinen, bis ich werde,
zieht mir das weiße Kleid nicht aus!
Ich eile von der schönen Erde
Hinab in jenes feste Haus
—J.W. von Goethe

That day I went to the museum of instruments –
remember their *jour fixe* afternoon
recitals? – how one time the pianist, a young Korean,

played the Diabelli variations with such pizzazz
and fire we were blown away by her?
A trans-Siberian spring wind was in force

that afternoon with its peculiar northern iciness
that slips its knife into your soul and grips the trees,
and drives the salt tears from your eyes.

I sat among the elderly widows who call by
the underground café to sip their solitary coffees
and peck at whipped-cream buns and apple pie,

perched on their chairs like well-groomed crows
before they flutter upstairs to the hall, pushing their way
with resolution through the dilatory crowds.

We'd often seen them and smiled at the flap and flurry
with which they settled on their front-row seats.
I've joined them now; it's the familiar story:

I'd been complaisant, smug, arriving late with you,
we'd lock our bikes outside and run into the hall,
you'd hold my hand while listening, my friend, my paramour,

my love. Troubled by lines an alto voice
sang at the concert, I wonder if that winter night
you too had wished to hurry from the beautiful earth

down to that firm and sombre house
to rest a while and then to waken with unclouded sight.

You didn't say – it's been so cold and silent since you died,
and no replies from you, no answers, only silence.

A line by Borges

was in my head *when sorrow lays us low*
as I walked across the blond fields of Brandenburg
in late summer, *when sorrow lays us low.*

The fields were cleanly shorn already
like boys way back in primary school.
I thought, I must tell you about this, about

the sorrowful eyes of Borges and the consolation
of a face given back to us in dreams of which
he spoke and which I've come to know painfully well.

I thought of Borges' eight million Shinto deities
who travel across the earth, touch us lightly and
move on. The year had reached its tipping point,

the light was brushed already with a hard
late summer brilliance that foreshadowed its decline.
Below me where the cropped fields sloped

down to a hollow lay a meadow pond,
neat as a silver coin amidst unruly
grass and nettles. It seemed

the sky had funnelled itself into it,
surrounded it for contrast with a ring
of dark-leafed trees, poplars and willows,

and sent the glass-winged dragonflies to flit
above the water like child's play or laughter
hunting for their prey, a cruel scene of gladness;

and who released the legion of swallows
swooping from high beyond the trees?
Which unseen hand pulled the strings? There was

no sound, only a far-off tractor growled in triumph,
I was at a loss, the plainsong of the waking earth,
its music had gone silent in the face of carnage.

Then I recalled the poet's lines – we're saved
by gifts of memory, he'd said, by a beloved face
returned to us in dreams or by some modest Shinto gods

who touch us fleetingly
as they continue at their ease across the earth.
That day laid low by sorrow in late summer

I thought of you: as long as I can talk to you,
I thought, you will not leave,
as long as I can dream of you, you will stay.

Left-handed

On our walks along the pier or by the sea,
you'd always take my right hand with your left, casually

putting it in your left-hand raincoat pocket
enclose it with your hand and hold it as we walked.

Nothing has ever felt so right again. We'd talk,
you'd keep my fingers warm or stroke

my thumb with yours, you were left-handed,
I loved your hands, I'd read them, every detail,

the lines, the scar left by a cut, the freckles, nails, the veins,
I'd study them, measuring them against my own,

I knew them like the back of my own hand.
So often we would round the long pier's end

turning back to the low grey town, its brooding sky
where we had landed for our sins so many years ago,

between a lake, a river and the sea, the "northern Venice",
with its copper-rusted dome, its lit-up clock face

that counted out the hours of our days
and mostly got them wrong. You'd hold my right

hand in your left and keep it warm inside
your raincoat pocket. The days were often blustery and wet,

the winds were wild. And yet
I felt an unseen gracious force around us that

seemed to make my steps so effortless
and gravity-defying. How presumptuous

I was to think I'd an exclusive privilege.
Perhaps the gannets and the crows that rose

cackling and cawing from the water's edge,
perhaps the passers-by, the solitary men

out with their dogs, the children on their skates,
the efficacious women on their evening runs

could see my lack of foresight, read the warning signs
I didn't see: my carelessness,

my mounting overdues and bills
I owed for happiness; my credit slashed to nil.

Graveyards

1

In the past when burial grounds were overcrowded,
the coffins of the poor were stored on the branches
of graveyard trees. They awaited judgement day
on swaying perches high above death's
teeming marketplace. Dignitaries or the wealthy
purchased plots close to a cathedral's inner sanctum
to ensure an expedited salvation. A grave
in sight of the altar cost several pounds of silver,
directly beneath the altar gold.
They lie under grave slabs whose emblems,
numerals and letters chiselled for eternity,
have been worn away by countless feet,
sinking deeper into the ground of the nave.

2

In the second year, due to overcrowding
in graveyards, we bury the dead
in makeshift graves excavated in parks, clearings, pastureland
or in improvised cemeteries, in mass plots
where hundreds lie under nameless stones,
unidentified and unclaimed.
They have begun the slow descent towards
nothingness, their names will not be found
in hospital archives, and their relations wander
rows of identical graves finding no trace of them.

3

My love, on a cold grey January day,
we buried your ashes beneath two stunted thorn trees
in the graveyard of outcasts – a ghetto garden
above a bog-brown lake ringed by dark mountains.
Here lie the nameless, stillborn, and unbaptised babies,
victims of hunger and typhoid, suicides and strangers,
on a slope beneath mounds of moss-covered stones –
a company, I know, you would have chosen yourself.
The small, crooked white thorns shadowing your grave site
were almost stripped of their scarlet berries, their gift
to birds who are the world's gardeners without borders.
We brought you here, to these lichen-encrusted thorn trees
and buried you beneath the rough grasses.
After rain, small white waterfalls poured themselves
from the mountain slopes and the lake's alchemy
turned them to gold in its depths. You were at home here
where a greater love had said, this earth
is all my children's in rain and silence;
this field of moss-covered stones, thorn, and bracken
remembers everything, forgives everything.
Nothing much blooms here and the flowers are small,
their colours so intense they are a blow
to the heart, the heart that's like a tough small horse
leaping and pounding the ground with its hooves.

Quartzite

In January's rough weather I went west to your garden
of the dead. The wind had swept across Connemara
ferrying rain, and clouds hung dark against the light
that streaked the hills with glints and lit upon
wet quartzite rocks half-buried in the weather-beaten slopes.

No lack of water in this sodden place, the country
drenched and dripping, river and lake overflowing,
and I was on my way to you with three quartzite stones
picked up on the gravelled path.

They'd shone like the white pebbles in the tale
of two kids lost in the woods, and I was Hänsel,
sure-footed as a somnambulist,

I knew each tree and gorse bush by the river
whose amber-coloured water I must never taste
lest I'll forget, or so it's said round here.

That day I'd found the wooden bridge gate padlocked.
Could this be the work of Uriel? Why is there always
someone who must take control? It's as the poet had it,
half the world loves, the other hates.

I climbed the gate and waded soaked to my ankles
to the grove of ragged hawthorns, stones and moss,
where I stood long beside your grave
on which, sunk deep into winter grass,
stood a girl's head a friend had cut from stone,

rough quartzite which he'd carved and polished
till her brow and forehead shone.
I caressed the head, discoloured now
with streaks of moss, blessed it for watching over you
in this remote, storm-blighted place. Perhaps the dead
cross easily between their realm and ours

and come and go again, just like the flock of dunlins
I'd seen earlier on the shore who rise as one
and vanish as they turn before the light
and turn again and as by magic reappear.

I laid the quartzite pebbles on the stone as it's done
to keep the souls of those we've lost with us
and in our world – to hold them fast by longing
and by being longed for.

Great Loon

I heard its call, its wake-up call:
three wailing notes from way beyond
the misty lakes, the place of myths,
the northern world that's slowly slipping its moorings.

One dreary wet day I heard its forlorn wail on the strand:
the chilling notes of a flute
cut from an ice-cold bone.

It told me that no one and nothing endures,
not you, my love, and not even
this grey sad stretch of water
nor the small damp houses that pretend to be cheery
with their out-of-season roses and Jack Russells.

And although the call tugged at my heart to breaking
point, I stood and wanted
to hear it again and again

because no one would teach me
this lesson so well,
in so few piercing notes, so little time.

By the Estuary

Years ago. That first sunny day after weeks of rain,
wind talking to itself in lilac trees and rose bushes,
our table with a view of the estuary –
transatlantic light,

the river and the incoming tide working each other
in a glitter of rival currents
and the resident heron rising on powerful wings,
ponderously gaining speed across the water,

fresh mussels in a bowl, white napkins and wine –
did I make all this up? Our old friends
who took up the conversation
where we had left it off twenty years earlier?

Did I sleep on that green bench under the Scotch pines
with my head in your lap?
Tell me, my love, weren't there two wicker armchairs
and a breeze riffling through the unread newspaper
almost bearing it aloft like a smudged herald?

And it could have, for all we cared,
and taken its bad news with it, do you remember?

Was it true that a sun ray struck a kayak
and turned it into a small golden-oared vessel
before it vanished in the darkness under the bridge
and faded like a memory?
And was there a kite sailing the clouds beyond the river
with its delicate rigging and tail?

Did no one warn me how fleeting this was?
Did no one say this moment
in which you delight is already lost
as you will achingly learn?

The outwitting eye sees quicker than reason
can measure, and though the heart
lives in terror of sudden rents
and tender words are spoken
in fear and trembling,
it soldiers on with its given unmerciful task.

Night Train to Bucharest

We never arrived in Bucharest,
although our pre-war carriage
was sign-posted PARIS-BUCURESTI.

Remember the old woman in our compartment
who was going home to Bucharest? She kept slipping off
the worn plush seat during the night,

flung onto the floor by her nightmares.
Please, believe me, Madame, I said, helping her back
onto her seat, *there is no more Securitate.*

Two Moroccans in the next compartment
fed sticky baklavas to the children. Their small red
transistor radio played mournful melodies till morning.

We were carried across the dark continent
to the sound of inexpressible yearning.
The night withdrew as day took the first

light steps on electric wires, daubed
a glint on the rim of an oil tank. We never arrived
in Romania, we were scattered in all directions.

But what if we had woken up in Bucharest?
Would we have had *cafea cu lapte*
in the station bar in Gara de Nord?

Would we have gone back to our other lives
in the Armenian quarter?
Would you still be there with me?

Valentine's Day

Some moments stay in your mind –
caught out of the corner of the eye
as you walk down the street:

a young father on the subway
with a baby strapped to his front,
tenderly protecting her head with his hand,

a black-cloaked man spitting phosphorous flames
on the main square. Sometimes an instant
so startling and singular leaves you to wonder

if it hadn't been a dream,
like that evening in a strange city
when from a rained-streaked bus window

I saw my doppelgänger stride along in a halo of hazy light
and cross the road into her other life,
and once on Valentine's Day

an encounter that struck me to the quick
so I ran home to tell you about it,
forgetting you were long gone:

a man had propped his mobile phone
up on a discarded roadside shelf
and, as I passed him in the busy street,

I saw he was talking in sign language
with a woman who was signing back.
They were in love, even I could understand

the words he conjured from the air
with sleight of hand and set them flying:
they were the metaphors of love,

hearts, golden apples, silver apples, roses,
he showered her with flower petals
and she received his gifts with open hands.

We, too, are condemned to silence, my love,
but don't you see how eloquent I am
with my hands raised, signing and signing to you?

Cold Spring Haiku

FESTIVAL

Chilled to the bone I see
the sun dance across the field –
a warm-up juggler.

DISCLAIMER

Pink buds. Apple trees
carry their spoliation
inside them like frost.

FOG IS A ZA-ZEN CONDITION

Dense fog. The midlands
are more radiant in fog
so Zen scholars claim.

SUNSET

Swallows whirligig
on their playground in the sky
mythic golden field.

SIGN

A rusted red gate
flanked by hawthorn in rich white.
Beware of the dead.

GARDENS

Trees tall as bastions.
Below branches in spring light
no shadow of you.

Memorandum

Jawohl, sie sind nur ausgegangen,
Und werden jetzt nach Hause gelangen,
O sei nicht bang, der Tag ist schön,
Sie machen den Gang zu jenen Höh'n!
—Friedrich Rückert

This is to tell you that your desk is as you left it:
papers, notes, your computer turned off,
Don Juan in tatters, and your beloved Heine, the worse
for wear with marginal notes, loose pages, dog ears,
still open at a favourite
passage. And while I pace back and forth
thinking how the earth
has tilted towards disaster and how glad
I am that you're not here to see it, I turn
to your Heine to feel the warmth of his words.
God will forgive me, that's his job, he said.
You'd often read his poems out to me, saying that
his laughter was wrested from a heavy soul.
Maybe you've just gone for a stroll
by the canal. Did you not promise to return
when the storm's died down?
Your reading glasses on your notes
still magnify the words *silent world*
in your neat handwriting. And underneath:
Goodness is a vast country. Wherever that
might be is written in the stars. My love, I've read
about a legendary city on a hill.
A wall of sorrows cuts across its heart
and separates the living and the dead.
People slip messages between its stones
where the shadows linger. I'll put this with the ones

I've left before, hoping that someone
beyond the wall might pass them on.
I have so much to tell you still. It's said
that sometimes late at night, voices are heard
whispering the pleas and promises
found there. When you've read mine, please
take them to the riverbanks, take them
and bury them beneath the weeping willows.
Please, bury them tenderly
beneath the weeping willows.

Jammertal

Ich bin der Welt abhanden gekommen.
—Friedrich Rückert

in memory of my brother Gerhard

He will always be young, my older brother.
I am long past the age he was the day he died
when his heart had struggled too hard against
its sad weariness and gave in,

when I looked for him and found him
alone in his room with the sun and the dust motes
dancing indifferently above him,

when the police and the doctor came,

when he was loved by us
and many more, his students, his musician friends,
his car mechanic, his tax accountant, and even
the middle-aged woman at the check-out
who was devoted to him,

when he was sovereign of the floating moment,

when he set his wristwatch to his own remote
time zone as inaccessible as outer space,

when he composed *divertimenti*
for street noise and starlings,

when the linden trees at his window
unstoppered their perfumes for him in June nights,

when the world's most beautiful alto (Janet Baker)
carried him off to the land of summer moons,

when he wrote poems in microscopic script
on stamp-size paper,
miniature time machines that ticked and chimed,

when his brief cryptic messages
were the wit of the soul,

when he was king of the smoke rings that rose
and were transubstantiated into revelations –
a daily miracle in his kingdom,

when he was as free and easy
as the ash tree in the park, the tree
that housed insects, crows and the stars,
in whose shadow old men played
the world's slowest chess games,

when he became lost to the world more and more,

when he slept with his head on his radio
and the sorrow of Bruckner in his ear,

when he was told in his dreams what music is,

when he came home from work
unspeakably tired that day,

when he lay down to take a short rest
that lasted forever,

when I found him and my first thought was
that he had hurried ahead without waiting for me
while death tinkered with his stopwatch,

when the emergency team, the doctor,
and the police arrived in force,

when they trouped into his room
with their paper authority, their instruments
and official stamps and their minds made up,

when we stood in the hall
unable to speak or move,

when they closed the door
and shut us out,

when they went to work in there
purposefully as frost,

when they carried him out
in a black plastic sack,

when his T-shirt and jeans lay on the floor, cut in half.

Autumn Alphabet

in memory of my brother Frieder

I see my brother, seventy years old and more, sprint
through colourful autumn woods. It is the season
of spiders, spinners of silken wheels.

My running brother has plugged his headphones
into his language app: he is learning Hebrew,
alef bet gimmel hey.

Sometimes he speaks the answers to the prompts
or he just listens. Other days he learns Arabic,
thā, tā, bā, khā, hā, jim,

the languages of two desert peoples mingle
in his kindly, humorous soul.
He calls me *habibti.*

I see him between the trees, years after his death,
running through the forest,
running past the river falls,

past yellow and russet trees strung with glinting orbs
spun by the goddess of weavers,
his life receding behind him like the bright wake of a boat.

He flies over asters and asphodel meadows,
growing smaller, fainter, harder to make out
in the distance of seventy and more years.

Tenderly, the spinner sun weaves above his greying head
a word made of Hebrew letters: אַהֲבָא *ahavah* –
a word made of Arabic letters: يبح *habibi* –

Tattoos

in memory of my granddaughter Ruby
April 30, 2003 to May 4, 2022

for Miriam

I

Did you know then, just weeks before your nineteenth birthday,
as you rubbed disinfectant onto the inside
of your friend's wrist, dipped the surgically clean needle

in India ink and, applying it gently
and taking care not to cause pain, pierced
the skin with its point again and again with

a steady hand, releasing the ink
and progressing little by little until
the clear outline of a larger-than-life bee appeared –

B for Beatrice, Brianna or Bee –
then having wiped away the excess ink and cleaned
the finished image with alcohol, and repeated

the process on your friend's other forearm, drawing
a seated, cross-legged angel two inches
in height, bent over and resting her forehead

on her knees as though in thought, the wingspan
measuring three inches across – did you then know
that these winged beings would outlive you,

would move through the world, through the narrow streets
of your hometown and further afield
on a young woman's warm breathing skin,

would be lifted in gestures of joy or despair, in dance
or the embrace of friends whom you had once
called your friends, too? How could you have known it

when you gave these tattoos as a gift for life,
inscribed with the clean lines of ink onto skin:
a namesake and a guardian, two messengers

taking wing in the growing light of spring days?
You couldn't know we would have to mourn you,
much too soon and without warning

leaving us helpless, unable to grasp
your sudden death, because this
was not supposed to happen – not this – none of this.

II

We were so many in the ICU it was a wonder
the hospital staff didn't fret and ask us to leave
and it was a wonder we didn't wake you

the moment we were allowed in and gathered round you.
The ICU ward's silence pressed on our ears, our hearts,
a silence broken only by the rhythmic sob

of the ventilator breathing into your lungs.
It was a wonder we had hope still, gazing at you
while the monitors flickered, your life support

scooping you up and lifting you elsewhere:
Snow White lying in a deep dream on snow-
white pillows, with your black hair and delicate face,

the endotracheal tube in your mouth, the ward an array
of glinting steel, monitors, oscillating graphs.
And while we stood there, your voice

rose suddenly like a wonder and filled the room
from a phone your mother had turned on to play:
a song we'd heard you sing not long before

with your own warm breath, your fingers picking
and holding down the guitar strings, your arm slung
casually round the curved body of the instrument.

And now we're here beyond the unit's door, lost and bereft,
all of us who loved you. We are tattooed now
with the permanent ink of grief

that penetrates past skin into the heart,
etches its sign, and colours all the world,
the same world that had opened up to you,

displaying the sweetness of its prospects
for just one moment
before slamming shut again.

You were nineteen that night of CPR and ambulance
and doctors in a rush that's just a blur in our minds.
Often I think of the Sybil now

we'd seen with you in Paris at an exhibition
six months earlier on a screen.
She danced outside her cave among the whirling leaves

inscribed with people's futures which she sang
in her strident voice while reading from the leaves.
We should have listened to her, but we didn't know.

If she had picked a different leaf for you,
what would her prophecy have been? Would you have
been given a chance, would you have been granted life?

Sightings

...lift up your grave and walk.
—Tomas Tranströmer

for Ruby

There are small things in nature we take comfort in, sightings,
signs we're perhaps foolish to think you sent us,

so now that you're not here to see it I must tell you our denizen
    blackbird
made her nest yesterday in the clematis by the back window,
    ignoring
my presence in the garden, she swooped in and out of a thicket
    of white blossoms
with grass in her beak, then settling in and turning around, her
    flirtatious tail bobbing,
she shaped the nest with her warm body for the second clutch
    of blue-green eggs,

and on a warm April day walking with a friend by the banks of
    the Corrib
a bat looped from the treetops with her little creased mask and
    tiny fangs
and stayed high above us, testing the inaudible echoes
and tumbled and polkaed about overhead with lop-sided flutter
    and flap
then zipped across to a flowering cherry tree and was gone,

and last November I caught sight of the Great Northern Diver
    again, the dandy –
remember how we admired his ambassadorial gravitas – whose black-

and-white feather I'd picked up earlier, a gift deposited for me
on the estuary's shore – swimming low on the grey water
and lifting his regal head forlornly, calling and calling,

and last summer by the Landwehr canal bridge, a red vixen
     with her triangular face
and alert auricles stopped in the underbrush to scrutinise me on
     my bicycle
then pounced on a mouse and holding it dangling between her
     teeth –
a treat for the cubs in the den – she streaked, an orange flash,
     down the embankment
running alongside me before a thicket of willows closed around her,

and in March on a boat halfway to an island I saw a pod of dolphins
break the surface as one to the children's noisy delight: fifteen,
     twenty of them,
lifting their streamlined bodies into the air in one elegant arc,
     diving back
into the blue-black water, and surfacing again they played
     around the boat
escorting us all the way to the pier to the islanders'
     wonderment,

and recently not long after you left us a white butterfly, a Cryptic
     Wood White
or an Orange Tip, made a fleeting appearance in the garden,
blowing about like a shred of white silk and returning day after day.
I was told white butterflies carry messages to us from the dead
     and although
I could not quite believe it, tell me why my heart leaped every
     time it returned?

An Empty Barn in the Midlands

An empty barn in a sodden field filled with nothing but clouds
and sky, no more than a galvanised roof on four posts, open to
wind and rain. Was there no one to store a harvest beneath its
roof, the corrugated roof under its red blanket of rust? From
the train window I saw it standing alone in the field, and it
struck me how it was a monument to nothing, always waiting
for plenitude or to be given a reason why it stood out there in a
midlands field, just as the roofless temples on the barren
hillsides of the Peloponnese with nothing but the sky between
their broken pillars are waiting for someone to tell them why
and to what purpose these stones were hewn, squared and cut,
heaped and tapered. Was it to hold a tympanum or a frieze of
feasting or squabbling titans and gods, or to enclose a great
emptiness? Everyone and everything long to be accounted for,
even the barn, the corrugated iron, the temples, the hewn
stones, I thought, watching the emptiness of a world pass by
that was once filled with your gaze.

First Beginners

I dreamed I am going to school with the dead.
They are my teachers. Their faces are mostly stern
sometimes amused, sometimes
they tut-tut or shake their heads at my incompetence.

There is no schoolyard where footballs are kicked into the sky,
no choirs or assemblies. I have surrendered
my worthless degrees and joined first beginners
on mounds of cold earth.

Our lessons are hard – we begin with the basics: *yes, yes –*
no, no. We must believe the words,
recite them like psalms.

Later we are taught further details down to the last knife,
the surgery sutures, the dog leash,
the lack of love and the mortification,

also some moments of joy,
shocking as ice-cold water.

It takes a lifetime to graduate
but I am determined to advance quickly.

I'll get stars in the end, I'll be rewarded
with galaxies of stars.

Snow Owl

I have been living too far from snow. Here it falls
as water in solid drops that don't dissolve
at the touch of a breath.

This is a place of light swaying in sea caves. I long
for snow in drifts by the wayside,
its whispered cover-ups.

Here the streets are named after dead generals.
I feel like some forgotten oddity in the corner
of a bric-a-brac shop.

How I wish for the snow's silence,
its alert and godly cleanliness
that blankets my failures. The snow owl

on its silent flight through the snow
is a white-on-white riddle
that enfolds me with its gorgeous wings,

a welcome vanishing act –
its cruel beak
its golden eyes
its feathers falling like snow.

Three Questions, Berlin, November 2022

for Vincent

It was one of those early mornings
when snow falls like white confetti
and people walk the streets as though returning

from an all-night party, nursing
a secret wound. At dawn someone woke me
passing by under my window sobbing.

In the taxi to the airport there was a notice
on the back of the driver's seat.
It asked three questions:

Where do we come from?
Does life have a meaning?
Where are we going?

I was certain the taxi driver who was from Ankara,
in Berlin since '82, had the answers,
but when I asked him, he laughed and shrugged.

He had pictures of his children, a boy of nine
and a girl of thirteen, glued to the dashboard
and a plastic rose tied to his rear-view mirror.

He slowed down on Pushkin Allee
with its four rows of old plane trees.
Over time their top branches had leaned

closer and closer towards each other
across the street for support
till they formed a ribbed vault.

It was as if we were driving along the dark green nave
of a Gothic basilica.
The day opened its notebook

still unmarked by sorrows or delights.
Just for a moment it seemed possible
that the wounds would heal, the sobs cease,

the answers to the questions flash
for a blinding second
across the blank page.

Eclipse

But the darkness pulls in everything –
shapes and fires, animals and myself,
how easily it gathers them.
—R.M. Rilke

Not many are waiting this morning before sunrise
to be ferried either East or West across
the Stygian rivers of the city

and I hardly know myself what I am doing here
on this ill-lighted platform,
my hand with the Obolus deep in my pocket.

Why can't I be Orpheus, casting a spell on stag,
bear, tiger, snake or tortoise, and rouse
the sullen-tempered master of the Orcus with my song

so he'll allow me one more glimpse of you
who went ahead alone one winter night
and crossed the wide torrential river without me?

Pigeons dancing the foxtrot on the glass vault roof
to the off-key hum of the cool drinks automat
are my sole companions, they don't give a hoot

where I'm bound. The only other human face
in this underworldly station is pasted
to the back wall of a sandwich stall,

a life-size photo of a young woman;
a piece of blackened glass held to one eye
she squints at the sky. It's the 29th of June in 1927.

On that day a partial solar eclipse
could be witnessed in Berlin
the moon's shadow slowly moved across the sun

until a narrow sliver, barely a rim of light
was left, glimmering
like a vague unease. (Who knows, perhaps she thought

this was an omen, six years later
when the lights went out for a "Thousand Years"
in that doomed city?) And suddenly I am back

standing on the banks of the Elbe with you,
where a small ferry had emphatically knocked
all night against the wooden pier,

most likely as a warning – of what we didn't like to guess.
That day we'd been out walking in sunlight
and birdsong by the water

when a change set in, so slow and subtle that we hardly
noticed it at first – as if the afternoon
were dimming or something ashen were leaking into it

then the choruses in the trees fell mute
and groups of people stood, their backs to us
gazing at the sky through soot-black shards of glass

as a deep shadow spread and closed in on
the radiant day. We turned away and shivered
in the greyish light, the sudden chill

and silence – we were young
ill-prepared for omens
we had no safeguard and we dared not look.

The Singer's Fable

in memory of Mary McPartlan

When the singer left, her voice didn't leave with her, we still
have her voice. In it are the sounds of home, the smells that
kindness makes of bread-baking and coffee, and the colours,
the bitterness that sorrow makes. Broken sounds and sweet
sounds and sometimes the voice dances like a bird in love.

People fell under the singer's spell the moment they heard
her sing; it is the pure tone that goes straight into your soul and
turns on its searchlights. What it finds there I dare not think.
When she was small, she went running into the fields in her red
dress where the sheep stood close together like parishioners
listening, their heads raised to the sky, they wanted to join in.
They were awe-struck in their hearts.

She went to fetch water for her mother, the living water
from a well where the trees rustled all day; there was a wish tied
to each twig, each branch, there were hundreds of them, the
trees quivered with the wishes of the people. Her mother
washed her hair with the clear water from the well. The singer
descended from the bus in her childhood hippie colours and
long plaits to sing in the lanes and yards of a small town until
the people came out of their houses and listened.

She walked along the streets in the tallest city on earth,
singing as she went, was lost, and found again by a black jazz
pianist who said the sound of dawn was in her voice, the young
light of a new day with all its unshed tears.

They played together in the park between the catalpa trees,
they never stopped in the middle of an unsung song, their
music had the spring smell of wild garlic. A ring of listeners
formed around them, not one of them was older than twelve.
The light struck the ground, and the trees swayed like Talmudic

scholars at prayer, rearranging their *tefillin*, whispering their urgent psalms. The piano player and she sang of the abandoned synagogue, all forgotten now, wedged in between a Chinese dumpling shop and a garage, a home for pious spiders. They sang of nights in Soho, they sang the old songs.

The music was not about the dark times, but the dark times were in the music. Her voice broke down at barred gates, at grave sites, there were too many of them, it knelt in bombed-out homes, it wept over abandoned children and grandmothers in shattered kitchens. Why have you forsaken us? it asked from its kneeling ground. The question flew to the ridge of the roof where a fat golden wolf moon hung in the sky. We sit, all of us, in a circle of its light, fearful and silent, listening to the singer, we hear her promise and her plea: Join in the song, she says, all are needed to complete the chorus that no matter how off-key and harsh always returns to the true note. Sing, even if your hearts are heavy, even if your houses are on fire, rise up and sing.

Dvořák in America

Antonin Dvořák, composer from Bohemia,
walking with his viola by the Turkey river
that flows through Spillville, Iowa.

He'll soon stop to take out the instrument and play
for the scarlet tanager, calling to the elusive bird
who hides in a black willow
and it will answer him, stanza by stanza.

After the quartet is finished, the tanager's song
is in the trills of the violins and the composer's
response in the sweet, mournful solos of the viola.
America in 1893: Antonin Dvořák, emigrant, homesick

for the hamlets and rivers of Bohemia,
a man, straight as a tree
with an unruly beard and a gruff demeanour,

who loves his wife and nine children, pigeons and beer,
who carries his briefcase of songs with him
on steamships and westbound trains.

The melodies come flying in his direction
like the homing pigeons he loves: the folk dances
of his fatherland, the plantation songs
and the tribal melodies of the Algonquin,

which are sad, Dvořák says, sad beyond despair.
And his black friend Harry T. Burleigh, student at the Conservatory
who sweeps the halls to make ends meet

sings the old spirituals for him *very often*
and before he wrote his own themes.

The four strings tell us: if you want music that is heartbreaking,
tender, gay, pass by the grand houses
on your way to the shacks beyond
the railroad tracks. Look for it there

and in the choirs of the small wooden church
by the black willows where the tanager sings.
It will come to you in an Algonquin water song

sung while sailing in an open boat
downriver to the musical shores of Bohemia.

The Cardboard Suitcase

A yellow van idles across the street as two men unload a box.
Obviously, it requires the strength of two to lift it. No one is
home, so they haul it back to the car and drive off. I am
standing by the upstairs window expecting a delivery which I
don't want, but know is unavoidable. I must be there when it
happens, when the suitcase is brought, the shabby cardboard
case covered with stickers of dead hotels and filled with illegible
postcards and letters, war diaries, world maps showing
countries that no longer exist, the remnants of a time and place
inhabited by people in starched collars or herringbone corsets;
school reports, doctor's prescriptions, war medals, steel helmets,
uniforms, the photo albums with pictures of black and white
cities that have been erased from the earth together with their
populations, photos with scalloped edges of long-dead
neighbours and family members who succumbed to illness and
bombs. Am I expected to spend my time going through all this?
What on earth am I to do with the inherited misery of a
murderous past?

Eroica

Concert in aid of Ukraine,
Berlin, 6ᵗʰ of March 2022

Many of us are crowded into the Berlin opera house
this Sunday morning, not one of the red velvet seats
is empty. We've come to this three-tiered golden hall
for the consolation of music, our hearts
are heavy with the news of war.

It is back on our screens, in our minds,
detailed as a medieval canvas
painted in the bleak colours of soot, blood, and rust.

We've come from all parts of the city
whose streets and houses could tell us about it,
if they could speak: bombs, sirens, the park in flames
and thousands dying among the rubble
or running for their lives, backlit by fires.

We've come to listen to Beethoven's *Eroica*
in the hope that the music, the instruments,
the clarinets or violins will reassure us.

The old conductor is in pain, weighed down
with his task. He can hardly lift the baton.
Sometimes he directs the musicians with his eyes only.

We move closer together, we sit in a circle
of golden light, safe and fearful. We are no heroes,
but somewhere not far from us heroes are made.
A poet once said: Pity the country
that needs heroes, and we do with all our hearts.

How can music drown out the uproar of cannons?
And yet it does again and again, the violins
tremble in despair, the oboe sings,
the sweetness of the cello solo lifts us up,

all of us, as we sit there, the older man next to me
with his walking stick, the woman in front
who wept throughout the funeral march,

and the first violinist with her delicate face
who is working the bow
at breakneck speed.

The Earth Remembers

Standing on the verge of a bog in county Roscommon –
where half the population died
during the famine years –

we the indigent and needy and distressed

you close your eyes and see ghost cottages,
a row of them beside a hill:

humbly deprecate

thick walls of rough-hewn stones softened by moss
the gaping window holes ivy-wreathed,

having no means to procure a subsistence

you hear the grasses stir in a western breeze –

bear the merciless pangs of hunger

meadow fescue, tufted hair grass, velvet bent
and the delicate quaking grass –

the awful and melancholy state of these humble and peaceful people

and you imagine you hear them whisper the names
of hundreds, thousands,

give them work before they are exposed

this is holy ground,
wherever you go, you walk on a grave.

to the impending danger of present famine
which has neither shame or honesty

There is nothing to mark them,
just a few stones perhaps,

forgotten beneath a mound of brambles,
or between hawthorn trees,

but the earth remembers for you.

⁓

The image of the Yemenite child
lying in the nurse's weighing bag
hardly measuring a pound reminds me

of the angels' weighing scales for souls
on Gislebertus' tympanum in Autun, Burgundy –
souls found too light on judgement day were tossed aside

but this bag-of-bones child lies, a ton-weight
on my heart day and night.

⁓

The year's countless dead are laid out
in row upon row in parks, in fields, in wasteland –
vast makeshift gravesites

for mass burials in Cape Town, Sao Paulo,
New York, Djakarta, Vienna,
Bergamo, Kampala, Aberdeen.

The wind carries the scent of grave flowers:
it visits the graves with its offering of tormentil
bog myrtle, meadow sweet
golden bog asphodel.

Twenty-eight Swimmers

I see a beautiful gigantic swimmer swimming
naked through the eddies of the sea
—'Song of Myself', Walt Whitman

The young men glisten'd with wet, it ran from their long hair,
Little streams pass'd over their bodies.
An unseen hand also pass'd over their bodies
—'I Sing the Body Electric', Walt Whitman

Twenty-eight swimmers in the Libyan Sea and a hundred more,
twenty-eight swimmers in the Tyrrhenian Sea
and a hundred more and hundreds in the Ionian Sea
and more in the Aegean,
their ships turned over, the boards cracked
and the rusting hulls broken apart by the weight of hundreds
and the engines stalling and sputtering
and running out of fuel
the boats adrift in the night
and the storms that sweep them overboard
and the dinghies and rowboats alone and lost
in the vastness
and everywhere the beautiful swimmers
in international waters and in the Marmara Sea,
in the waves and under the waves, their bodies glistening with wet,
little streams passing all over them,
the bodies of women, of mothers, of sisters and daughters
and the bodies of young men and old,
brothers and fathers and sons and none of them known
by their names, not by a single name,
little streams passing over them, over the long thighs and slim feet
of the young men, the young women,
over their strong courageous arms,

the delicate necks and chests,
the waves cold and salty, and a hundred more afloat
on their backs with their bellies swelling to the sky,
over the children with their slender wrists and arched feet
adrift and rocked in the billowy drowse that swings
and sways, bangs and bruises and sweeps them aside,
the sea that is neither friendly nor unfriendly
passing over their limbs, their bellies,
their faces and heads with the tight wet curls,
with the streaming long hair, with the sleek hair
stuck close to the skulls and faces,
the sea rocking them in its billowy drowse or dashing them
with neither loving nor unloving spray,
the sea that is wide as the world with shifting
horizons, breathing its unceasing broad
and convulsive breath, the sea
that is heaving with always ready graves.
How you, singer of the sea, would have cried over
and mourned for the beautiful swimmers
that your hands could not pass over with love anymore,
that no one's hands could pass over anymore
with love or kindness, the swimmers with their courageous arms
and urgent legs, their breaths becoming one
with the spume and the water and the swift-running eddies
which they struggle against steady and long.
How you would have called their names, a name for each of them,
how you would have wept over the brave
beautiful swimmers who were rolled and swung,
turned and finally dashed against the unwelcoming rocks,
swept aside and borne out of sight.

*It is estimated that more than 28,500 people have died
since 2014 trying to cross the Mediterranean Sea.*

The Soul Model

Yael Bartana's video installation shows cars cruising along a three-lane highway, the ones in front entering an underpass then slowing down and coming to a standstill, the drivers and their passengers getting out and standing beside the cars in complete silence for two minutes. It's Yom HaShoah, Holocaust Remembrance Day. Take the whole blue earth into your soul today, the trillions of details and fragments, watch planes and clouds converge, cruise ships as tall as houses nose around narrow harbours, there's so much of it, crisis meetings, eclipses, tears, joys, illnesses and rhetoric, the years measured by the incremental growth of children notched in red marker on the doorframe: *(Tom, aged nine in socks, Lily, four, standing on Shakespeare, Emma, 14, in high heels...).* There is such abundance and dread we stand silently with sad hearts and awed, we contain galaxies and subatomic particles, nebulae and the blindworm in our minds, prison yards, memories of school days, knives and violets, the grim daily fog of routines and the exultant music of dawn choruses, the rare silk of sunrise – as one of the year's emergency conferences gets off to a bad start – loving gestures and automatic rifles, a young woman wipes her baby's face quietly singing; in the Danish fishing port of Skagen boats set out at first light on an empty voyage on an empty sea, a young man listens on TED to a noisy discussion about the lack of silence in the post-industrial world, a busker on Potsdamer Platz plays Vivaldi's Four Seasons on his accordion to the plugged ears of the passers-by, the spires of Bohemia reach for the sky glinting in the sun and daisies growing from a crack in the underpass tremble in the breeze. In Tajikistan a thousand-year-old Buddha measuring thirteen meters in length lies asleep, resting the cheek of his great face on the palm of his hand, his sacred footprint is preserved at Sri Pada on the island of Sri Lanka. A British artist has made a model of her soul; it is a white translucent tangle of synthetic material, elastic, weightless, gleaming with rapture. Some imperil their lives so that others can flourish, their faces in newspapers on screens appear pixelated, vague.

Kindness, my father said, can be truly heroic and asks for nothing in return. He knew the truth of it: someone had saved his life in the Judean desert once, taking great personal risk. Let the masters over life and death reconsider, let them put down their instruments, the blades, gavels, and guns for two minutes. Let's all of us stand outside our lives in silence, let our souls go over the four corners of the earth singing.

The Great Weights

Among the clutter on my worktable, a stone
serving as a paper weight. I had picked it up

from hundreds of similar stones on the ground
in the latrine at Auschwitz-Birkenau.

It is a flat, ugly, grey stone, no bigger
than a man's palm, an irregular triangle

with rounded edges, one corner chipped,
leaving a gash, its surface worn

by the feet of those who suffered
and those who inflicted suffering.

I had to summon all my strength
to pick it up from the ground of the latrine.

On the way back to Berlin it lay
heavy in my pocket although

it was only five inches long and three across,
this stone with the scar on one corner.

Every day I look at it weighing down
the papers on my desk.

Every day it teaches me a hard lesson:
Remember not to forget.

Early Morning

See this woman at sunrise who watches
the shifting light and shadows
on the curtains of her bedroom window.

The early sun paints the wooden frames
of the small square windowpanes
onto the white linen curtains,

a spreadsheet into which the morning
will set the agenda
for another day of grief and longing,

taking care not to omit
a single bullet point of pain
between alpha and omega.

Behind moving clouds the grid appears
and fades, lights up and vanishes,
the alphabet comes and goes,

the chambers of the unflagging heart
close and open
close and open.

Dear Jessie, when I think of us, how young
we were! If only

we could have just another one or even five minutes of those days,
(but let's not be greedy), when our hair was blonde or red or
    black and our dresses
were loose and light, six of us or more, a circle of friends in the
    lamp's glow
inside a lit-up circle of words, the streets in our small town
wet and dark, the day tasting of rainwater and salt.
I'd love just one more of those days that weighed light,
with us arguing about nothing less substantial, nothing
of more consequence than a line in a poem – an obscure or
    jarring line,
or a word picked up on a street corner or left behind
in a rumpled bed, an appeal stuck to a mirror, a word
birthed by a clammy sea like a bag of sludge, a word
that took to the air like the kites the kids let fly
on the swamp near your old house. We sailed
in that rickety boat of language, and you'd be the one
setting the sails with the calm assurance of a mariner.
Jessie, forgive me, in a watery city like Galway
where the sea rises a little each year
the nautical metaphors are plentiful as flotsam found on
    Grattan Beach.
I remember your loose-fitting dresses you'd cut out from patterns,
fusible, interfacing, wide trim and flap and single fold,
poplin strewn with flowers, lawn, linen, spotted silk;
there was as much finesse and craft in your dresses
as in the complex patterning of a verse, and I used to imagine
a poem that came easy, a poem I could live in
like a favourite dress, something light and loose.

When I think of you now so many decades later
up in your clifftop aery,
where the rockface below you is patterned white
with the gentle streaks of bird shit left by world-travelling birds,
I see you walking with your trusted sheepdogs
more a flock than a pack in this windswept precipitous place
with puffins and kittiwakes, razorbills and guillemots for company
as well as the odd fiach dubh, the stern priestly raven
cruising the thermals or winging it back to his nest of sticks.
Dear Jessie, we owe you a lifetime's gratitude,
you built your house of poetry with love and persistence over
    the years,
made from patterns of words, of lines that connect worlds,
a house with room for many to live in:
welcoming, spacious, airy, light.

for Jessie Lendennie

Where Music Begins

Consider this: you are at the edge of a cliff and your task is to leap across the void onto a safe landing place opposite you. You must land firmly on your feet [...] and pick up the same speed you had [...]. Too short a leap will have you dashed on the rocks below. Too long a leap will have you flat on your face [...]. This is a fermata in music, a magic moment when there is an enormous build-up of tension [...].
—Micheál Ó Súilleabháin

Berlin in lockdown, the concert halls deserted,
pianos on stages standing in half light, lids closed,
fallboards down. There's a quarantine silence
in the city's streets and squares,
and to defeat it a young man has invited the world
into his room where he will play the Sonata for Hammerklavier,
written by Beethoven in anticipation of a gift,
a piano from London, sent to him by master piano builder
and devotee John Broadwood. The young man
has set up his camera and microphone and now
he begins with those seven chords
that fling the doors open into the first movement.
We don't know what music is, but we understand
that its need for freedom is unrestrainable,
it sets out to roam far and wide, sometimes stopping
for just a few moments at the edge of a cliff
before taking a wild leap across, landing
with precision and ease on the other side and
gathering speed from there to its destination
in the ears of listeners where music begins.

II

Twice being labelled an "enemy" lost my father two pianos.
Back from the Great War, years of saving all he could
from his meagre pay had bought him the first one,
a third-hand concert grand; it had a sweet, light touch, he said.
When the brownshirts came for him, the "enemy of state"
who loved Schubert, Bach, Chopin, he left it behind and fled.
Years later, deported from Jerusalem, he lost the second,
a baby grand he'd bought from a colleague,
an "enemy alien" like himself. Fingers press the keys,
hammers touch the strings, the mechanism sets
the notes in motion. The music is transparent, flowing
like the amber-coloured bog stream beside which I stand
watching its progress downhill from one chatty waterfall
to the next below the bridge where the meadow pipit
takes a dip. The river is so clear each pebble is visible
on the bottom, and now and then the silver flash of a trout.
The night my father died, Schubert was on the stereo,
the Sonata D-960 in B-Minor. *Molto moderato.* He'd played it
the day before on his Steinweg, his third and last piano.
The final sense to go is the ear, I am told.
How much did my father hear in the end, I wonder,
did he hear the notes streaming over granite boulders
to the turn in the river where the moorhen nests?
Did he hear the skylark rise up fast and straight
from the marshy ground into the sky singing,
unable to contain the joy in its small heart?

i.m. Micheál Ó Súilleabháin

Evening on Three Bridges

The rain always knew where to fall, and unlike us
the river was never riven by doubt where it should go
as it rushed headlong into the bay.

We woke with our faces still far away in our dreams.
When we went outside, we saw the wind
stop by the trees on its way inland
and salute each single leaf in turn.

The seaside houses were small and sleepy-eyed
with half-shut blinds;
every human-made thing was modest
and the church on the pier could easily fit into a toy box.

We loved the mornings when the face of the town
was freshly scrubbed and everyone
was already up doing their job:

singing to itself the sea was busy
lacing and unlacing the moorings
of the boats in the old harbour,

starlings cleared away crumbs around coffee tables
or picked up the odd errant snail,
and cormorants sternly patrolled the estuary.

The largesse of the sky knew no bounds here;
at a whim it brought forth rainbows
or downpours that fell slantwise
across the town like beaded curtains

and the clouds hoisted their topsails and cast off
heavy-bottomed as caravels.

In the evenings the piscatorial college
whose door frames were made of whale ribs
was brightly lit up. Behind the windows
students sat at study bowing their heads
over charts of the ocean floor.

At nightfall we would walk seven times
across the three bridges of the town,
hand in hand with our memories.

Someone will write us into a book
and give us new names.
Someone will write until their wrists ache.

The Fox

for Richard

lifts a paw and pushes and the earth turns
till it reaches a small village
between mountains.

That's where the fox wants to go. He leaps –
and vanishes
on a blank piece of paper

on an old poet's writing desk.

In the Second Year – from a Pandemic Journal

Silence is a word which is not a word,
and breath an object which is not an object
—George Bataille

A love-breath that takes you to infinity
—Rumi

And in this harsh world draw they breath in pain.
—Shakespeare, *Hamlet*, Act 5, Scene 2

I pray so my soul can breathe
—Billboard, Berlin

Music is the poetry of the air.
—Jean Paul Richter

Music is the best consolation…
—Martin Luther King

Fill your words with the breathings of your heart
—William Wordsworth

Reading the news during the past months – wildfires, floods, wars, the pandemic and its daily statistics of death – I recalled my six-year-old granddaughter asking me years ago, will there always be enough air? will it run out? worry creasing her forehead. Our train had stopped next to a water-logged field where the reeds stood in tight bundles like fasces. On journeys we often talked about topics that troubled her. What could I say? that in many places on earth it was getting harder to breathe? I told her, no, that could not happen, unsure if what I said was true. Look at the sky, I said, its deep blue colour is no more than air, trillions of air molecules carrying short waves of light. Astronauts tell us seen from space our planet is wrapped in a diaphanous blue layer of air we call the atmosphere. Air surrounds us; it is vital for all life; it can be wild in a hurricane and gentle in a breeze; it strokes our hair, our faces; it is buoyant, holding us like water and carrying us when we fly high above the clouds. When we are glad, we dance on air, when we're afraid our breath stops; a flower, a face can take our breath away. The clever swifts can sleep in flight resting on air, and the best gliders of all, the seagulls, ride the thermals without moving a wing. The minute you were born you caught your first breath and you haven't stopped breathing since. You laugh and cry, speak and sing because you breathe. We can study what air is, what gases it contains and their names, its molecules and atoms, and how it enters our bloodstream and makes us live. We gather knowledge but we don't know the cause of it all, we don't know why. No one knows the answer to that question.

A few weeks ago, I had sad news that a friend had died from pneumonia; her lungs had filled up with fluid, leaving no space for oxygen to sustain life. In her last minutes her exhalation was so faint, a leaf placed on her lips no longer trembled, the mirror held up to her mouth did not mist up. I try not to think of her in the ICU, her lively spirit drawn towards that moment when we return the breath we had fought for on entering life, fetching it deep into our lungs and exhaling in a cry.

Of all instruments, she had loved the wind section most. Around the time she died, as I found out later, I was listening to eight young musicians play a serenade for winds, the sweet oboes and flutes flying high as though airborne above the horns and bassoons booming along in the bass line, pompous and jovial as 19th century bourgeois. The eight musicians filled their lungs and blew the air through narrow tubes made of brass, silver, ebony or rosewood; the melodies followed one after another lightly, cirrus clouds drifting in the blue overhead.

⮌

Months after life in the city had been put on hold, I walked the streets at night and as I thought of the many fighting for breath in the ICUs, of the photographs of blue oxygen bottles, ready and waiting like miniature missiles and saurian-green excavators tearing up parks for graves, of the exhausted faces of doctors and nurses shrouded in pale yellow PPE, my eyes filled with tears. The world had shrunk to the size of a computer screen. During FaceTime my distant children, my distant friends were the size of passport photos signalling from far away. At night I walked under trees clad in their funereal garb of black leaves trying to comprehend how it was possible that a mere breath had become a potential hazard to others, how we were surrounded by this threat and our precautions so helpless. Perhaps the dead know more than the living? Maybe they drop urgent messages before our feet, but we don't see them. Maybe the whispering willows stroke them when they pass in their ghost chariots.

⮌

It's said the cavatina in his string quartet opus 130 moved Beethoven more than anything he had ever composed. He himself commented that he had "truly written it in the tears of melancholy". The cavatina travelled on the Voyager to the edge of the solar system as a gift for someone 'out there', in the hope they might listen to its melodies and shed tears, as Beethoven did, writing it. To the astronomer Sagan, the Voyager's photo of the earth showing our planet as a pale blue dot was an illustration of the folly of human conceits. The drums of my neighbour's nocturnal techno music are like the regular and syncopal beating of a heart. When it stops, I lie awake and worry about him. In this second year of the pandemic, we concede victory to 'an organism at the edge of life' we neither see nor know. Now even two-year-olds are dying from it, the delicate tissue of their lungs ravaged. Often when the constant beat stops behind the wall, I think of George Floyd's heart-rending gasp, his breath brutally crushed out of his lungs under a policeman's knee, I think of the *Seven Last Words of the Unarmed*. In the morning the workmen restoring the house opposite are back behind the green plastic hoarding. They are hardly visible, shadowy and active like stage actors at rehearsal or poltergeists or my beloved dead.

Quintilian taught Roman schoolboys the art of rhetoric. Speaking well means speaking justly, he said. Gifted orators adapted their speech patterns in such a way that whenever they needed to take a breath the concept expressed came to a natural conclusion as if by coincidence. Similarly, when a musical phrase comes to an end there is a pause, sometimes hardly noticeable, sometimes pronounced. For just one moment the musicians lower their instruments, their trumpets, oboes and clarinets, they lift the bows off the strings, the violins off their shoulders, even the drumsticks of the kettle drum are held aloft and still. According to Quintilian, the moment when speakers or budding orators have wound up a proposal is also the moment when they must hold still for a second or two and inhale. They might keep their hands raised during that short time or allow their gaze to range over the listeners, trying to overlook the woman in the front row who has fallen asleep and is gently snoring. This is also the instant of inspiration: a new thought is born and immediately the speakers are off again until the next breath pause. Or so the teaching goes. But this ideal of a mutual physical rhythm of speaking and thinking doesn't work in poetry. The body is subversive, it mutinies, it won't obey the dictates of rhetoric; poetic speech is often fragmented, the lines are broken or of different lengths, breath rhythms may accelerate and become irregular. The more heightened and contradictory the emotions, the shorter the lines and the speaker's breath. We cry, we laugh, we sigh in pain. The body breathes rapidly, it is winded, it hyperventilates, pants, sighs, gasps, spits out words and phrases, often it runs out of breath. Language becomes pure sound, the poet's speed increases, she must move fast to keep pace with the poem that runs riot and overtakes her. Her heartbeat tries to keep up: da dum, da dum, da dum, da dum, da dum. Some poets have a theory that all human hearts beat in iambic meter – da dum – and a line of a sonnet with five stresses is equal in length to a breath. All day long our hearts beat, *The curfew tolls the knell of parting day, Shall I compare thee to a summer's day, Errichtet keinen Denkstein! lasst die Rose, With how sad steps, O Moon, thou climb'st the skies!...*Sonnet rhythm is innate in our bodies, we walk and breathe to an inner beat, all a poet needs to do is to work magic and translate it into words and images.

⁀

Two years before his death, my brother gave me a recording of Beethoven's late quartet, opus 132 in A-minor. *Listen especially,* he said, *to the third movement: Molto adagio, A Convalescent's Holy Song of Thanksgiving to the Divinity in the Lydian Mode.*

Beethoven lived two more years after writing this music in which people claim to hear the voice of the divine. The Holy Song of Thanksgiving was written in intervals of recovery while Beethoven was near death from an intestinal illness. At the times when he felt well enough, he would work on it. It wasn't completed until after his convalescence. Anyone who listens to this music will find it difficult to describe. It is the heart of the quartet and must be played very slowly: *molto adagio*. It evokes the convalescent's gradual return to life, the pale blue light of early morning, open windows admitting clear air into the sickroom, the sounds of horse-drawn carts on cobbles outside, firewood being chopped in the neighbour's yard and Dr. Braunhofer's reassuring tread on the stairs. The Lydian mode Beethoven used, however limited, traditionally expresses joy and feelings of gratitude. The Song begins with a handful of notes that pass slowly from one instrument to the next, like a message passing from hand to hand. The strings sing these few notes hesitantly, quietly at first, then they become more and more forceful and high-spirited. We know they speak of Beethoven's gratitude to the deity for his recovery because he told us: *Doctor, close the door against death. Notes will help him who is in need.* But there is more, and maybe those listeners are right who feel that the music is from another world. It's as if Beethoven meant to comfort us who are so in need of comforting in our captivity.

A friend writes to me about feeling lonely, about the endless empty days of the quarantine. Not a soul has come to my door for weeks, she says. No one, not even the turf man. Sometimes the postman carries his bag past her house and up the road to another address. Lately she has been seeing things. On

76

Valentine's Day people passed in the street wearing red hearts on their sleeves. Once a masked face was pressed to the window glass. When she looked again it was gone. She dreamed of someone arriving from a long journey. How she'd welcome them! And the miracles she would work! They would wake up the next morning with the walls and doors of the house gone, the slates lifted off, Cassiopeia and the moon settled on the roof beams, lavender shooting up blue as gas flames through the floorboards, the garden a riot, birds singing at night. What a party she would have, the starry carpet rolled out for all her neighbours and friends who call to the garden fence with roses, music, dogs, and wines.

En plein air – this is what the artist wants us to see: a portrait of himself in the open painting air. He wants us to understand his dilemma – how do you make the immaterial visible, how do you paint air? Although we don't see it, it fills so much of the painting within the painting which is still in progress we can see the canvas billow like a sail, hear it creak and breathe. The sun is high in the sky, we know that because the artist himself and his few painting paraphernalia as well as the canvas on the easel throw short deep shadows from left to right. He has portrayed himself from behind on his knees in his tartan shirt and battered hat, we see the soles of his heavy boots on which he squats, to his left the box with tubes of paints, turpentine, rags, brushes on a four-legged stool; he kneels on the sand which is pale yellow, the same colour that fills part of his painting at an oblique angle and which he is busy applying to the left-hand corner at the bottom. His hat is pulled down over his eyes against the light that keeps playing tricks on his vision. We think we see what he sees, the wide expanse of strand with tufts of dry dune grass growing here and there, we believe we can hear it rustle in the sea breeze. Beyond the strand stretches the deep blue band of the ocean, and above it the unbroken lighter blue one of the sky. If it were an abstract painting it would consist of three horizontal bands of colour. Dominating the centre right is the canvas at an angle screening part of the scenery from view, breaking the near-parallel lines of sea, strand, and sky. It shows us the artist's vision, he invites us to share in it quite literally. But he sees more, further, deeper than we ever will who are destined to be at a distance behind his back forever. We can never approach close enough to look from the height of the dune down to the waves rolling in, nor would we see the glitter of sea foam on the crests, the dune grass bending over slightly in the wind if it weren't for the half-finished painting. The artist on the other hand will never come to an end, that's his fate. He will be working on his difficult task forever, held fast in time trying to capture the transient light, the moving air, the moment that is already past.

⁂

Sometimes in the blue hour of dawn when the blackbird's song raises the shutters on another day, the city draws a breath and exhales, like a sigh of sorrow perhaps or relief. I hear it amid the slow airs of coffee shops waking up and arranging their offerings of pastries for sleepless angels. A sudden gust shakes the trees, seeds helicopter elliptically to the pavement. A red squirrel crosses the path and disappears in the undergrowth. A little later I see it sky-vaulting mid-air between the higher branches.

⁂

The Brodsky Quartet played the Cavatina in one of
Amsterdam's Prinsengracht concerts, standing on a light-strung
pontoon in the canal, the audience seated in small boats or on
the banks hardly moving as if holding their breaths in their
unsteady crafts – the video clip shows their faces: one man has
tilted his head far back to catch every single note the grachten
air carries towards him, a couple sit in a motionless embrace, a
woman's eyes are filling up with tears. This was recorded a few
months before my love died in the darkness of a winter
morning and two and a half years before the pandemic stopped
all music across the world, two and a half years before a
quarantine silence took over the streets and concert halls. Then
music returned step by step, first in the open air, a guitarist on a
balcony, singers gathering in front gardens along a suburban
street, a solitary violinist on a hospital roof above Cremona
playing Gabriel's Oboe to clinic staff, and one afternoon in
Dresden's district of Prohlis atop the highest tower blocks an
orchestra of wind instruments, sixteen alphorns, nine trumpets
and four tubas plus percussion and drums, let fly with
Palestrina and The Sky above Prohlis, fanfares and dances, the
alphorns calling for all the world to hear and the people twenty
and more floors below them in the parks or on their balconies
forgot about their sorrows for a time, the stealthy illness and
the many graves. Later the musicians of the Dresden symphony
joked it was like Mont Blanc up there, the air clearer, more
bracing, the sky a much deeper blue.

A friend once told me he never mastered to breathe properly
while swimming, although as a child he'd practised holding his
breath for as long as he could. When his beloved died, he
dreamed of her swimming upriver as she left him, her family

and friends; waterborne, free of pain at last and breathing freely she swam, he said, under the Pont du Diable and vanished at the line where water and sky become one. The memory consoled him in his grief. I told him about a video I had seen that made breath become visible: a camera focused on an artist's lips, behind her face a light aqueous blue conveying tranquillity, dreams, then almost unnoticeably the image dissolved as the lens misted over. It was like the ultimate test in reverse, the mirror held up to the mouth, not of the dead but of the living; the artist had breathed new life into the concept spiritus. One single breath of the divine inspired a figure shaped from a lump of clay to rise and draw his first lungful of air. By contrast, there is another realm of air, the nebulous, cloudy, the dream from which half-formulated ideas slowly emerge into the light and take on contours, become finished, fixed, acquire an aura, become art.

⤳

I wonder if anyone else has an ear so tuned and sharpened as I have, to detect the music, not of the spheres, but of earth, subtleties of major and minor chords that the wind strikes upon the tree branches. Have you ever heard the earth breathe?
—Kate Chopin

A drawing of a small piece of our tortured planet, twenty-five square inches of acidic meadow: tough little leaves, hard grasses and the blossoms as fragile and precise as if they had been copied from a medieval painting. A botanist would be able to name each plant and tell us that bird grass, field-woodrush, couch grass, rushes or sedum, and miscanthus were here long before us. This drawing is more than a copy of nature. It draws our attention to that which carries and holds and nourishes us, not a divinity but simply the earth, the soil that is crisscrossed and bound by living threads, a root system that seems chaotic in its random tangle. From a lump of black clay grow these graceful and vulnerable structures. When I look at it closely, I imagine the earthworm at work in the middle of it. There is nothing commonplace about grass. Its biological diversity is breathtaking, its adaptability seems infinite, its capacity to absorb and convert CO^2 into oxygen by means of photosynthesis is miraculous. Without grass there would have been no air for us to breathe. Grass possesses an astonishing vital energy and dynamism which manifests itself in the most delicate forms. This drawing of a square foot of meadow with all the clay still stuck to the roots is not only physical and tangible but also metaphysical: it is no mere replica of reality, but a dreamscape, visionary and of unearthly beauty.

⁀

When I was a child of six or seven my father would often bring one of my older brothers and me to small towns in our district that had survived the war more or less unscathed, towns with narrow crooked lanes, a market square surrounded by splendid patrician houses and a large city hall. Usually there would be a tall old church, sometimes even a cathedral at the top of the square. We'd enter the dusky interior and climb the stairs to the organ loft. My father was known in the district as an organ player, and he had access to the instruments wherever he went. Often these were built by famous organ builders of the 17th or 18th century. He would open the manuals and if the mechanism of the organ was electrically powered, he'd pull out various stops and registers listening to their tones before he would launch into a prelude by Bach. But it could happen that air supply to the organ had to be manually operated. In that case he would ask my brother to work the bellows that regulated the wind pressure which enabled the organ to produce sounds through its many silver pipes. There were two bellows mounted either to the side or the back of the organ with a weighted lever on top of each that had to be lifted and allowed to sink down again. This operated the blowers and caused the air to flow into the organ's wind chest. My brother would lift first one of the levers, let go of it and lift the other one and so forth. It had to be a constant, uninterrupted and rhythmical motion causing the organ to come alive, breathe and sing. I sat beside my father on the bench while his hands worked the manuals, his feet moving from left to right and back on the wooden keys of the pedalboard that my feet couldn't reach yet. I was allowed to pull out stops that changed the colour and timbre of the music. The names of the stops he taught me were *Carillon, Cuckoo, Prince of Flutes, Glockenspiel.* Once my brother stopped working the levers of the bellows, the air flow would also come to a stop and the music fall silent. My father said that the Latin word for bellows was *follis* and that the Italian word *folle* meaning *fool* came from *follis.* He said that we were like bellows and fools, full of emotion and air, fanning flames, speaking, singing, making a sweet or harsh music just as an organ does. Take the air from it, from us and there's nothing but a dead silence.

⤳

Even the clever animals sense how defenceless and
out of place we feel in our decoded world.
—R.M. Rilke

During the first year of the pandemic when the streets were empty of people the animals left their lairs, nests, holts, hutches and dens, their hives, burrows and beaveries. They came down

82

from trees, mountain slopes, meadows, they crept out of forests and the undergrowth, they came from deserts and wilderness, from mid-air above the ocean, from the ocean, from rivers and lakes and from the depth of rainforests. In great numbers they streamed to the places they usually had shied away from. It was like the days of the ark, except this time we were the ones to be rescued. They came to our big cities and small towns full of wonder and interest, they came to wherever we were, sitting inside our houses full of fear, wherever we had covered the living earth with walls, stone, fences, and tarmac. A puma padded down a main thoroughfare in Chile all silvery pelt and fluid movement, small grey monkeys played and leapt at traffic junctions in India. Penguins waddled undisturbed through the art museum in Kansas City. There were sightings of orcas gathering in Scottish waters, flamingos in Mumbai arrived in such numbers the river turned pink, wild goats ate the well-fed grass of the suburbs. Dolphins were diving and swimming close to harbour walls in Italy and rare sea birds arrived in Venice. It seemed that wild creatures had come to reassure us they were here and ready. The foxes had long been their vanguard in the cities with their clever pointed faces and their alert auricles always vigilant, living and operating under cover of darkness. We are here in our dens, I wanted to say, waiting for the time when we, too, can glide out, our eyes on our tracks like you, our noses to the ground like wild dogs. By the end of the second year, we have been turned into fabulous creatures with strange names: unicorns, griffins, phoenixes, basilisks, manticores. Our lives and yours are akin, even if they are separate and alien, you and we are as fragile and resilient as the other, we need each other. An enraptured peacock fans out his improbable tail feathers and dances an awkward lop-sided joyous dance. Why is it that in the middle of trembling we want to sing? Why although wingless do we want to rise above the earth and sing?

⬥

Fujiko Nakaya has devoted her life to remaking the world from no other material except clouds, fog, mist, and haze. Her father was an expert in snowflakes, ice flowers and crystals, so it is natural that she continued in the family tradition from an early age, studying how to make air and water become physically tangible and miraculous. Her father told her that if you wanted to understand ice you had to listen to it whisper and sing. She took it further and learned to listen to clouds. Clouds are like us, she says, they are born and die. During her long life, she has become a sculptor of clouds, making her luminous shapeshifting installations with the help of a machine built by a magician physicist. She is the only woman in the world who can make the essence of wind perceptible. Her cloud sculptures are alive: to the weather, the breezes that shape them, the sun that burns through them, they are impermanent like the Zen monks who dance in and out of the diffuse light between her fog towers like shadows, materialising for a moment and vanishing again. In Fujiko's incandescent house fog rises to embrace me in welcome. She takes me on a walk across a fog bridge and past the pond where the mist wafts and hovers above the surface like her own breathing spirit. I follow her into her fog garden, I go astray in crafted nothingness, I have no choice but to entrust myself to her lack of guidance. I have lost my passport, my face has disappeared from screens, it's become a blind spot on the biometric eye of the security camera. I am outside the law. The fog grazes the brown grasses, gets snagged on thorn bushes and climbs into the treetops. It slides down the tall buildings and enters them creeping through windows and keyholes, curls up and goes to sleep like a large soft animal. Slowly I unlearn the habit of seeing, I say goodbye to the world of things. I am a child released from school in winter fog country with my hand on the shoulder of the child next to me who holds on to the child next to her as we pass into a shimmering otherworldliness that has its own rules and resists all dictates of dimension or gravity. Fujiko Nakaya says only children and very old women enter her cloudscapes gladly without faintheartedness or bewilderment. For a moment I see her standing between trees in a haze of green, a small woman in her late eighties caressing a branch, tiny droplets misting up her glasses.

In the 1830s, Doi Tushitsura published two books of his nearly two hundred drawings of snowflakes. He named each one: snow flower, toothed flake, peony snow, ice dragon. When the thermometer was below freezing, he was outside bent over his microscope drawing the most evanescent thing on earth: frozen water-filled air. He found the flakes to be simple yet complex crystalline shapes, each single one following the same basic pattern, but each unlike any other, unrepeatable, an accident of formation created by air, water and temperature: prisms, needles, columns, plates from which delicate branches sprouted that vanished at a breath. While he worked, he covered his mouth with a scarf so his exhalations wouldn't destroy his samples. His books sold in their thousands and snowflakes became all the rage in Edo, their filigree forms appeared on kimono fabrics and green teacups and filled the cosmos in Utamaro's Floating World woodcuts as symbols of the brevity of life. Zen scholars meditated on the snow's beautiful ambiguities, how it yields and hardens, how it appears in soft and crystalline form. Tushitsura's drawings were records, memorials, the colours white and grey, snow and ashes. I had found his books in facsimile in an antique bookshop in Berlin-Charlottenburg. During the pandemic I thought of Tushitsura's snowflake drawings often as countless lives vanished around us as if they had been blown away. On one of those quarantine days in winter I was on a lake island in Berlin as snow began to fall fast around me muffling all sounds, only the flakes sang their inaudible high-frequency song as they drifted past me. Snow melted on my lips, my eyelids, cold drops ran down my face. The longer I stood enveloped by snow falling in thick white flurries, the more I thought I saw you in a waking dream, my dead loves, your barely visible shadowy forms among the dancing flakes that fell into my eyes. Were you here to ask me why I was not with you, why I still went on living and breathing? As hard as I tried I couldn't have answered that question. All I had was my breath that came and went and the dark clapper beating inside me.

www.ingramcontent.com/pod-product-compliance
Lightning Source LLC
Chambersburg PA
CBHW030501100426
42813CB00002B/298